THE BIG CHILL

DENNIS LOY JOHNSON

THE BIG CHILL
THE GREAT, UNREPORTED STORY OF THE BUSH INAUGURATION PROTEST

DENNIS LOY JOHNSON

MELVILLE HOUSE PUBLISHING
HOBOKEN, NEW JERSEY

Book design: David Konopka

Melville House Publishing
P.O. Box 3278
Hoboken NJ 07030

mhpbooks.com

Photo courtesy of AP/Wide World Photos

First Melville House printing 2004
Printed in the United States of America

ISBN: 0-9749609-7-7
Library of Congress Cataloging in Publication Data on file

FOR VALERIE, OF COURSE

THE BIG CHILL

Marquis de la Chesnaye: Corneille, arrêtez cette farce!

Corneille: La quelle, Monsieur?

—Jean Renoir, La Règle du Jeu

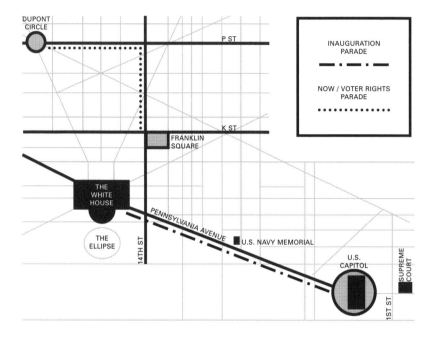

1

ON THE CORNER OF
14TH AND PENNSYLVANIA

The inaugural parade was late. We knew from radio reports that the ceremonies making George W. Bush president had ended long ago and still there was no sign of the presidential motorcade coming down Pennsylvania Avenue. We'd been standing for hours, packed together too tight to move in an icy rain, people terraced on bleachers behind us and perched above in the frail city trees, the endless chants long gone inane, the bone-chilling cold taking us from chattering optimism to a shivering hopefulness to a grim and feverish zombie determination... when a rumbling, off in the distance, became noticeable, then discernible—like a revelation—as something human. The roar came toward us quickly, sweeping along the steel-railed barricades lining the avenue, a chant you felt before you heard, a sound so vituperative it was startling, even amongst the vociferous—except then we could see what had caused it, and all the sodden and benumbed stupefaction of that disparate mob stripped away in a galvanic surge of anger. Everyone—the kids, the boomers, the old lady pressing on my left—suddenly throbbed forward against the barricades as one, with fists shot overhead in a massive group reflex, to shout—to scream—"Shame! Shame! Shame!"… not at the presidential limo we'd been waiting for but at the unexpected vehicles preceding it: two large, flatbed trucks filled with journalists.

They were, under the normal conditions of all the preceding inaugural parades during the last half of the twentieth century, supposed to be crawling along at a snail's pace immediately in front of the presidential limo so that the journalists could broadcast to the world the triumphal accomplishment of another leadership transition—the very triumph, that is, of democracy. A no-brainer of a job, really. Keep the camera trained on the big car. Let everyone see the long shot of the crowd smiling and waving, the presidential arm stuck out the window waving back. Watch, especially, for the part where the president gets out of the vehicle to promenade with the new First Lady and a First Child.

Except this time the journalists, standing there on display in the raw air on the back of those trucks, had their video cameras lowered, their telephoto lenses and their notepads lowered, and they were making no pretense of filming the motorcade now trailing distantly after them, nor the thousands of people screaming their hearts out at them—at *them!*—nor of filming any of the surrounding scenery, although it was all the stuff of astonishing and historic imagery—the massive and colorful crowd in electrified tumult against the backdrop of the gigantic gray federal buildings of our nation's capital; the lines of policemen standing shoulder to shoulder before them, five rows deep, with a row of trench-coated marines behind that, narrowing each side of the avenue; the mounted police in baby-blue helmets lined up behind the platoon of riot cops in full gear that were gathered at the cross streets; the military helicopters swooping low beneath leaden skies, or hovering ominously at a standstill; the sharpshooters lining the surrounding rooftops—the

United States Department of Commerce, the United States Department of the Treasury—like so many hostiles on the ridge.

This is what it took to get the new president from the Capitol to the White House.

But the journalists were recording none of it. Instead, they were standing there, bug-eyed and paralyzed by the immense and pounding wave of hatred from the mob. They hunched behind the slatted sides of the trucks, clearly aghast and terrified that what was probably the largest gathering of police and military ever in the nation's capital—the lines of cops and soldiers and horses and barricades and sharpshooters—was not enough to hold back that crowd of normal-looking people gone ugly with outrage. The speed with which the trucks were moving emphasized their air of desperation—they were racing toward the safe area a few blocks ahead, the area between the White House and the Treasury Department that had been cordoned off by large cement barricades and high wire fencing and more cops and military. The compound was closed to citizens without the right paperwork, which is to say people without an invitation showing that they either had made a significant donation to the president's campaign or were senior officials of the new ruling party.

But Pennsylvania Avenue between here and there was now a cacophonous gauntlet, the crowd stoked after being partly disheartened by the long series of buses that had preceded the press trucks—official guests being transported from the secure zone of the inaugural ceremony at the Capitol to the secure zone around the White House—buses whose esteemed passengers had variously hung their heads out the window to curse at us, or waved extended middle fingers or taunting three-fingered "W" salutes.

Equally deflating was the ever-increasing display of police and military personnel, so extreme as to seem unreal at times, like standing on the set of a Costa-Garvas movie about some foreign coup d'état. At one point, incredibly, a sailor even strode by against the olive-drab background of the Marines opposite us, his uniform popping-white through the gray mist. Periodically, too, there was a parading of the riot cops—their every surface molded with padding so that they resembled the muscular robot superheroes of little boys, with shield braced in one hand, baton at the ready in the other—double-stepping in ominous meaningless-ness down the block and back. Each time they were shown to us, I wondered if others around me had listened to Washington's deputy chief of police, Terrence Gainer, on National Public Radio's *All Things Considered* program a few nights before, giving the program's millions of listeners a long, soothing explanation in which he repeated several times—his voice mellow, more like that of a thera-pist than a law enforcer—that although a significant turnout of demonstrators was expected, his men would be wearing "soft hats," rest assured. Gainer had repeated the phrase insistently, as if it had real significance—*soft hats*—then clarified flatly: "We won't have riot gear on."

They stood now, dozens of them, futuristic gladiators, in front of the horse soldiers just off the intersection, tensed and ready after the howling at the press trucks, their helmets and shields gleaming in the incessant rain.

It was mid-afternoon and, thoroughly drenched, most of us had been there for hours by that point. The group I was with—three other fortysomething New Yorkers—had been there since noon, having arrived in the city to find most other events had been stifled. We'd traveled with a group intending to join a demonstration organized by the National Organization of Women and a nonprofit group called Voter Rights, to be held at Dupont Circle, one of only two locations, we'd been warned, for which a permit to demonstrate had been granted. The other permit had gone to a contingent of African American groups for a gathering on the Ellipses, who were having a separate rally to protest the exclusion of so many black voters from Florida. The Dupont Circle gathering was to culminate at ten o'clock with a march that would join the two groups at the location expected to draw the day's most sizeable crowd of protestors—the Supreme Court building ("the place where American Democracy died," one of the get-out-the-protest websites called it). Given what had happened, most people saw the march on the Court as the day's most significant event, a vital counter to the day's other significant event, the swearing-in ceremony taking place at the Capitol building. But the march, too, we'd been warned about—it was the only march that legally sanctioned to take place in the capital that day, so you protested elsewhere at your own risk. We were given a handout about what to do if arrested, a document that made a lot of the people on the bus, those who'd never done anything like this before, rather nervous.

But our bus had been blocked by police from leaving us off at Dupont Circle when we got to the city, even though there was supposed to have been a designated area for buses. Instead, we were diverted to the parking lot of RFK stadium, the football stadium outside the city, a considerable distance away, where we disembarked in a sea of buses from around the country that had been similarly diverted by the authorities, and from there, we were all on our own to figure out the Washington's Metro system and find our own way back into the city.

So, we were well over an hour late by the time we got to Dupont Circle, and we hustled through the park looking for the march. What we found were clumps of stragglers stretching from the Circle down to 14th Street. The march, we learned, had been broken up—inexplicably to everyone we talked to. People who had remained at the Dupont Circle rally told us the march had indeed started, with a packed Dupont Circle having emptied into P Street and filling it with people for as far down the avenue as you could see... but then it had just stopped, and eventually everyone gave up and wandered off. A few people told us they'd heard the police had stopped the march, which, as the march had been sanctioned by the police, was a bit ominous. But nobody seemed to know for sure what had happened. People with transistor radios said there was nothing about it in news reports.

Meanwhile, marchers and others who found their way to the Supreme Court building on their own found themselves confronted by a line of policemen closing off the sweeping steps aproning the building, where protestors traditionally gather, and by a wall of huge red, white, and blue buses sealing off 1st Street, the road in front of the building. This left only a sidewalk as a gathering space, and thousands of people were being kept out of that area and turned away by more cops. The towering buses, meanwhile, also blocked guests at the swearing-in ceremony taking place directly across 1st Street at the Capitol building from seeing any of the protest—or the suppression of the protest—going on at the Supreme Court.

At the other end of the inaugural parade route, around the White House, was the area—block after block—that had been cordoned off to safeguard the invitation-only inaugural partying. And the length of Pennsylvania Avenue itself, from the Capitol to the White House, was sealed off by stone and steel barricades and those lines of soldiers and cops. This also rendered Pennsylvania Avenue an impassible border zone that prevented demonstrators at the only protest rallies for which legal permits had been granted—the one at Dupont Circle organized by NOW and another organized by several African American groups on the other side of Pennsylvania at the Ellipse—from joining forces. The NOW march down had been intended to do just that on its way to the Supreme Court; but apparently, even if the police hadn't stopped it, the day's only legally sanctioned protest parade had been given a permit for a route that could not have been successfully completed in the first place.

Meanwhile, running a block parallel to Pennsylvania was another wall of stone and steel barricades; to get close enough to Pennsylvania Avenue simply to view the inaugural parade, people had to funnel through a handful of heavily manned checkpoints, where, under the observation of numerous police officers and various and sundry other unidentified security agents (usually, large men in small suits, with earpieces), any signs involving sticks more than three-quarters of an inch thick were confiscated, all bags were searched, and anyone arbitrarily considered suspicious was frisked. It was the first time that checkpoints had ever been used along the parade route and, mysteriously, many of them—and they were few and far between to begin with—were shut down hours before the parade began. As a result, the one left open at 14th Street, where my friends and I got through, had a waiting line that was blocks long and sidewalk-to-sidewalk wide. Ultimately, untold thousands were kept away from seeing the parade. They were left to wander an unfamiliar landscape in search of an open check point (the 14 long blocks from the Supreme Court to the open checkpoint at 14th Street, say) or, if they found one, they were stuck waiting for hours to get through.

Still, the crowd that did get through was enormous, packed tight into every available inch of space, overflowing the sidewalks and traffic islands and cross streets for block after block, as far down the avenue as we could see. The discomfort was intensified by the wicked cold rain, but people kept their spirits up through hours of chants. Those who hadn't had their signs taken away—that is, those with placards small enough to be held with their hands— waved them at the cops and each other, as well as at the numerous large men with earpieces and looking uncomfortable in casual wear who were spread throughout the crowd. The signs for the most part showed a good-humored sophistication: the single most prevalent was "Selected, Not Elected," but there was also "Re-Elect Al Gore," "Don't Blame Me, I Voted With the Majority," and "Clarence Thomas: The Only Black Vote That Was Counted." On the periphery, two men dressed like giant bananas strolled around and waved to passers by, and explained to anyone who asked that they were symbols of America's new status as a banana republic.

So despite the conditions there was at first an effervescent quality in the air, as if everyone was relieved and delighted to find, finally, other people, and lots of them, willing to talk about the large, dead elephant that had been in the national living room for months now. What's more, they were doing something about it, and in more ways than one: Early on, led by a mysterious group of black-clad, ski-masked agitators calling themselves the Black Bloc (who had first come to fame as leading players at the Seattle protests against the World Trade Organization), protesters took over the bleachers on the swatch of greenery behind us, a large traffic island between 13th and 14th Streets called Freedom Square. The bleachers were reserved for ticket holders—invariably, campaign contributors to the new president—and placed strategically to avoid giving opposition demonstrators a large, open space in which to gather. But few ticket holders showed up, and the ones who did left quickly when the cops decided not to make a scene by extricating the occupying army of raucous protesters, which included a boisterous crew with homemade congas. (The Black Bloc had, by then, vanished.)

The takeover invigorated the swelling crowd, which had started as pockets of special-interest groups, each bellowing their own chants in competition with one another. One group, for example, would chant, "Racist, sexist, anti-gay, Bush and Cheney go away!" while another group billing itself as the reconstituted Black Panthers chanted "Black power!" An anti–death penalty group would chant, "George Bush (beat beat) Serial Killer! (beat, beat) George Bush…," while the drums in the bleachers drowned out still another group in accompaniment. But soon, as the crowd grew thicker and thicker, and filled overwhelmingly with people who had no particular affiliation, it became evident that everyone was there for essentially the same reason, and the mob began to chant as one—although the more mature among us (about half the crowd appeared over 35) did defer to the younger element when it came to choosing the chants; they seemed to have a bottomless bag of rhythmically creative mantras. Each time the riot police were trotted out for a quick reminder display, for instance, the twentysomethings would point to them and chant, "*That* is what a police state looks like"—then point to themselves—"*this* is what democracy looks like!" It was so precisely and obviously true, and given such a catchy back beat, that the rest of us would smile and join in. One of the most remarkable moments of unity occurred when the miserable rain froze into a sudden pelting of hail; as one, the crowd, which was shoulder to shoulder and in the tens of thousands by then, broke into a spontaneous, rollicking chant of, "Hail to the Thief!" that echoed down Pennsylvania Avenue.

That ongoing rain and hail, however, had taken its toll over the hours of waiting, the crowd hoarsening and quieting and freezing, so by the time the press trucks suddenly appeared, and as they raced past, carting their occupants off into the blockaded secure zone, it was as if we'd gotten a shot of adrenaline. Everyone remained braced, then strained again toward the barricades, alert for the event they'd been waiting for. Shivering, suddenly, with energy instead of cold, the crowd's buzzing contained and amplified as it was thrown back by the helicopters that were suddenly hovering lower and lower, the scene combusted seconds afterward when the presidential limo finally came into view— behind, first, a quick fleet of police cars, each with their passenger windows open and a man in a suit running maniacally beside it as if his coat were stuck in the car door; then by a positively surreal phalanx of bright, white motorcycles molded together with equally bright, white sidecars, a huge chevron of perhaps twenty of them piloted by white-helmeted cops; then a wedge of black-windowed black sport utility vehicles, sliding along like so many Darth Vader helmets; and finally, amidst hordes of grim-faced Secret Service agents running flat out, their ties flapping—winded agents were replaced by others who suddenly peeled out of the many unidentifiable civilians milling amongst the cordon of cops and soldiers—came the black presidential limo, in a ragged, diamond-shaped formation with three other vehicles that were identical except lacking the presidential seal.

The still-reverberating chant of "Shame!" ratcheted into explosive, thunderous feverishness then, the kind of hysterical screaming where nothing else matters but the scream: "Shame! Shame! Shame!"; but it was as if that wasn't enough, and everyone, even the gray-haired matron beside me, who'd frowned at the kids doing it earlier to the press trucks, was now jabbing their middle finger—the only protest sign the police had left us—jabbing it at the motorcade, too, as if in desperation to show the true depth of outrage. It was a remarkable sight: As far as the eye could see, a convulsive sea of extended fingers stabbing the air, stabbing, as the cry went up and echoed off the huge stone buildings around us and as, swimming up from behind darkened bulletproof glass, the pale white hand of the new president waved at us in royal and ghostly oblivion, and sped by in a blur.

And then it was over. The racing chaos of the presidential motorcade had disappeared a block away, beyond the heavily guarded barriers where we'd watched women in fur coats and men in Stetsons entering earlier. People stayed up on their toes a moment longer, straining to see after the racing limos in the quickening hush, like a stadium crowd wishing a long fly ball into a home run—staring, as if that great cry at an onrushing car had to have some visible effect, and an abrupt quiet descended, and time seemed to suspend itself.

Momentarily, somewhere down the avenue, a marching band could be heard: the actual parade, but no one announced its coming—after a garbled sound check, someone in the crowd had pulled the plug on the PA system of the street-level announcer's booth diagonally across the street from us and the announcer (wearing, bizarrely, a white suit as if it were summer) had been pelted by so much refuse that the Secret Service had had to escort him away. But the distant blat of trumpets broke the spell, and the crowd settled; then slowly, uncertainly, began to disperse.

It had all come down to this: shouting and jabbing a finger at a speeding car.

Still, as people began to wander, their sodden miseries—I couldn't feel my feet, and it hurt to finally walk again—seemed forgotten; I realized we were smiling, strangers looking at each other, hopeful. In the resonant aftermath, the question was obvious: The powers-that-be had to hear that, no?

But who needs rhetorical questions? Hear it or not, I thought, wait until they see it in the next day's Sunday newspapers. The authorities had done a brilliant job of cutting down on visuals of any dissent: They'd kept permitted rallies to a minimum, then kept them separate and distant and unable to join one another, lessening opportunity for pictures of a large and integrated crowd; they'd closed off or severely restricted more pertinent areas that would have provided more profound symbolism, particularly the Supreme Court; and they'd broken up the lone protest march. By taking away sticks, the police had also prevented the stuff of more specific and vivid imagery, such as large protest signs and recently popular elements of street theater, such as giant puppets and stilt-walkers. Doing all this, however, had required such a huge police and military presence that there was no way, it seemed certain, to take a picture of the parade route without making our nation's capital look like a country undergoing a military occupation. And if those images looked half as ominous as they felt in reality, then a significant portion of the day's truth would thus be reported.

And then there was the image people would not see, the one that had led inaugural coverage for a generation: This was the first president since Jimmy Carter started the tradition* who was unable to walk the route of the parade celebrating his swearing-in. For modern presidents it is, perhaps, the transition period's most important photo-op— the new president steps away from the pomp and the isolated world of power to walk amongst the people. Of course, this president would have been mad to do so, given the size and ferocity of the

---

*After his swearing-in ceremony in 1976, Carter walked all the way from the Capitol to the White House with his wife and daughter.

crowd aligning the parade route. But that, of course, is precisely what made it a case of a missing picture's being worth a thousand words.

The stymied photo-op, then, was a recurrent topic of discussion on the late-night bus ride back to New York, and, despite treacherously icy conditions that made for the queasy sensation that the bus was hydroplaning all the way home, people seemed both exhilarated and relieved. No one had known what to expect when we'd begun the day—at 4:30 A.M., standing on the street outside Madison Square Garden while organizers shuffled us onto one of, by my count, 14 buses—but optimism had not been especially high, and the weather seemed certain to keep our numbers low, too.

But word on the buses was that the organizers were estimating that there had been an astonishing 500,000 demonstrators. And indeed, protesters had been everywhere visible in Washington, much more readily apparent—overwhelmingly so—than celebrants. In fact, to anyone simply walking around the

central part of the city, the most obv...
report was that, on the occasion of the inaug...
of our first appointed president, the nation's capital
had been overrun by people of every age and ethnic-
ity who were questioning the legitimacy of that
president—overrun on a day when the miserable
weather surely kept thousands more away. And no
one would have to take our word for it alone—the
best evidence that there were so many of us was the
fact that the new president had been afraid to get
out of his car.

So, even as people discussed how to capitalize
on their coming-together—there was talk of organ-
izing opposition to ongoing cabinet appointments,
several of which were felt to be proof positive that
the new president felt no compulsion whatsoever
toward the unity he'd apparently discussed in his
inaugural speech—there was a sense of accomplishment, and a tendency, at the end of that long
day, to savor instead what felt like victory.
Increasingly drowsy discussion kept coming back to

act that such a large
ted to protest not a war
tion of government. This
e told one another, and had
had started, and we had proof:
o, like the day itself, marked a

2 | ALL THE NEWS THAT FIT...

The impossible photo appeared in the Sunday *New York Times* the next morning. It took up nearly half a page: the new president and his wife, walking along Pennsylvania Avenue and waving happily to the crowd.

It appeared in accompaniment to *The Times'* lengthy lead news report on the front page, by reporters Frank Bruni and David E. Sanger, when the story jumped inside the newspaper.

Standing in my kitchen in my bathrobe, still groggy from the late-night bus ride, the tumultuous sights and sounds of the day before still reverberating through my system, it was nonetheless quickly obvious what had happened: Once the presidential motorcade had raced safely beyond the barricades into the invitation-only area where the general public was not permitted—the heavily guarded area where the press trucks had fled, and where we'd seen all those people in cowboy hats entering—the president had gotten out of the car and waved. Later, other newspapers confirmed the staging and filled in the details: He only strolled for a moment, they reported; just long enough for an Associated Press photographer to get the picture. Then he got back in his car.

In the *Times*, however, neither the caption of the photo nor the text of the very lengthy article it illustrated reported those circumstances. Instead, in paragraph 49 of the 50-paragraph article, it was reported, fleetingly and inaccurately, that the new president had gotten out of his limousine after it "had passed most of the protesters." In fact, of course, he had passed all of the protesters and was no longer in public, but virtually in his own living room. By failing to report that he was in a heavily guarded area before a selected audience of friends, family, and campaign contributors—that, as the *New York Post* reported, he was "in a secure, protest-free zone" where, as the *New York Daily News* noted, the crowd was "restricted to official ticketholders"—the *Times'* use of the photo acted to deny the far greater and darker reality of that parade route, and forcefully implied that this president had risen to the occasion in the expected manner of his predecessors. What's more, it indicated that the general public had in turn greeted this president as it had greeted those others—as Bruni and Sanger put it in their next and concluding paragraph, "Onlookers roared their approval." If you weren't there, you'd never know that the people Bruni and Sanger identify in such neutral terms as "onlookers" were actually invited "supporters" who were in effect "roaring approval" for themselves, and that the people labeled "protesters" actually made up the overwhelming majority of "onlookers" along the parade route—made up in fact, that day in Washington, the overwhelming majority of the public. It was another battering drill in what had become the lesson of the day: The majority doesn't necessarily count in a democracy.

43

And it was another dark moment from a Costa-Garvas movie: A staged photo had been successfully planted in our nation's most influential newspaper, where it was treated as genuine news.

But the fact that the *Times* relied on a staged photo as part of its coverage wasn't the only surprise that awaited eyewitnesses who unfurled the "paper of record" the morning after the inauguration. Even before arriving at the misleading photo of the presidential stroll there was the front page, which was, strikingly, dedicated in its entirety to inaugural coverage. It included more extra-large photographs complimentary to the new president— the new president kissing his mother, the new president dancing with his wife, the new president being sworn in—and three other articles of reportage and analysis... *not one of which contained any further mention whatsoever of the protests*, save for a vague, single-sentence mention in an analytical commentary by R. W. Apple Jr. of "an angry protest" by "the doubtful and the disenchanted." Beyond Apple's comment, and the brief and misleading comment at the very end of Bruni and Sanger's very long report, not another word in any of the *Times*' four lengthy, front-page stories was given to the thousands who'd gone to Washington to question the legitimacy of the new administration, nor to the unprecedented number of police and military personnel who'd been in the capital to greet them.

The elephant was back in the room.

Ultimately, out of the nineteen news articles concerning the inauguration that ran in its front news section, the *Times'* coverage of the protests came down to two more easy-to-miss mentions: A single-sentence reference, in a background piece buried on page 14, of a solitary Supreme Court demonstrator (giving no indication that there were thousands gathered there with him, nor mentioning the thousands more who had been blocked from joining them); and, on page 17, a 600-word sidebar about security measures, which described protesters not as oriented around questioning the new administration's legitimacy, but rather as confused and riven by "a variety of grievances." The sidebar was accompanied by a photo so small that it was difficult to make out its components. It was particularly difficult to discern the fact that, in front of the small crowd of demonstrators pictured facing the camera, the odd-looking round objects aligned three-deep along the bottom of the frame are the helmets of riot cops. Additionally, out of the 19 photos that accompanied the *Times'* inaugural coverage, this was the only one having anything at all to do with the protests.

In short, leafing through *The New York Times* the day after the 2001 presidential inauguration was, for someone who'd actually been in Washington that day, a baffling experience that quickly became eerie and even ominous: There was voluminous in-depth coverage of events behind the scenes, while the scene itself was largely ignored. For the *Times*, the day's pomp had been "news" (eleven photos of inaugural balls and the swearing-in ceremony), while the gritty reality of a badly stumbling democracy—the nation's first massive gathering to question the legitimacy of a presidential transition, to question not only the man but the process—had not. Certainly, the unsteady new administration, loser of the popular vote (at the very least and by the significant margin of over half a million votes), couldn't have asked for a more favorable portrayal. All the news that apparently didn't fit left nothing but a depiction of the transfer of power as smooth and widely accepted and having nothing about it that was out of the ordinary. Nor could the new administration have been displeased that this depiction appeared, no less, in what is unquestionably the most powerful news source in America, "the bell cow of the media herd," as William Greider recently put it. It must have also given the new, far-right fundamentalist Christian government pleasure to see this supportive depiction coming from a newspaper considered by most in America to be a liberal, Jewish bastion. (Although the *Times* had regularly run unfavorable coverage and been harshly critical of the president's opponent during the campaign, it had not, in the end, endorsed candidate Bush, although at that point it had seemed a fine point to many. Indeed, a survey by the non-partisan Pew Charitable Trusts Project for Excellence in Journalism found the *Times* and several other leading newspapers to have run more positive stories about Bush than Gore by a ratio of nearly two to one.)

Still, it was hard to believe that, influential or not, other news sources would follow the *Times'* lead on this one. For one thing, it was hard to believe that they would go to such drastic and con-voluted measures to avoid reporting information that pertained so directly to the fourth estate's most crucial role—that is, to report about the functioning of our democracy. And beyond such a fundamental ethical concern was that fact that the inaugural protest was, in the end, simply a good, juicy story, the kind of story one would think reporters would give their eyeteeth to cover—something historic and unprecedented and full of the kind of conflict, imagery, high emotions and large numbers that beginning journalists are drilled to look for. After all, in the entire history of the United States the actual transition of power has never before been protested, much less to such a degree that the Marines had to be called out.

But those were the hopeful thoughts of someone whose Journalism 101 class occurred in the heady days of the late seventies, when our scruffy heroes were famous for having dared to report facts that made the ruling powers look bad; when Woodward and Bernstein were held up to us as models of fearless investigation, and so was Dan Rather, whose famous exchange with President Nixon was something cool we would repeat to each other like a slogan.* But the *Times*' coverage made me nervous, and, still in my bathrobe, I launched an immediate search on the Internet to see what my other local newspapers were saying, and then what other papers around the country were saying.

I discovered that while most other sources had given greater attention to the protests and placed it

*At a televised press conference in March 1974, when Rather stood up to ask a question and received both applause and boos, Nixon snickered and asked, "Are you running for something, Mr. Rather?" to which Rather replied, "No sir. Are you?"

higher in their coverage (sentence number three in the lead story of *The New York Daily News*, for example), the *Times* was not alone in severely downplaying the size and nature of the dissent. Paging nervously through newspapers from across the country that morning, I found that reportage about the demonstrators was dutiful, at best, and minimal, almost without exception.

Nor was the *Times* the only paper that flatly misreported significant details to such an egregious degree as to constitute disinformation. Perhaps the most stunning whopper came from Doyle McManus, James Gerstenzang, and Nick Anderson of *The Los Angeles Times*, who reported in their page one story that "...at the inaugural parade, anti-Bush protesters were almost as numerous at some spots as Bush supporters...."

On the other hand, another of the country's leading newspapers, *The Washington Post*, detailed the "thousands of sign-waving protesters" in its lead story, and ran a photo of an injured protester, on the front page. In fact, the *Post* gave significant coverage indeed to events in its hometown: Altogether the paper ran four detailed and in-depth stories concerning the protests, including another on the front page, and six photos.

National Public Radio—also headquartered in Washington, and so also covering its local beat—ran several stories about or at least mentioning the protestors, including one report that detailed police beatings of demonstrators, and the fact that many were then detained and denied medical attention for hours. The leading webzine Salon.com reported that "demonstrators came out in droves," but "the police did an effective job" of keeping them off the parade route by "isolating protesters and the general public in small clusters." In New York, as mentioned, *The Daily News* and *The New York Post* gave fairly prominent attention to the protestors. And an impressively detailed story focusing on the protests also appeared on the wires of the Associated Press, reported by Ron Kampers (although I couldn't find any newspapers that had picked up the story in its entirety, or even in its majority).

But as it turned out, those were the exceptions that proved the rule: What ran in most newspapers had an eerie sameness to it. Most reported a record-setting number of "law enforcement" personnel, although that "record" varied between 7,000 and 10,000. Most failed to distinguish that this included not just police but also innumerable agents from the Secret Service, FBI, and indeterminate other civilian agencies operating out of uniform and under cover (the ubiquitous large men with earpieces), many of them taking pictures of the crowd with still or video cameras. Even more papers failed entirely to report the significant military presence. And no one at all reported on the discrepancies between public pronouncements beforehand by law enforcement officials on how they were going to behave—for example, Chief Gainer's promise that cops would show up in "soft hats" only—and how they actually were deployed. Nor did anyone report on the mysterious closing of checkpoints that kept tens of thousands of citizens away from the parade route.

If you were to make the logical assumption that there was a "record" number of "law enforcement" personnel because there was a record number of protestors, according to most newspapers you would be wrong, and by a wide margin: Just about everyone reported that there were only about 10,000 protesters present—a one-to-one ratio with the cops, in other words. What's more, these measly few were described—if at all—as predominantly young and mostly white. (Some said this even as they gave passing mention to the African American rally on the Ellipse.)

Just about everyone used the phrases *minor skirmishes* and *few arrests* (most reported 15). Other petty details were so commonly and bloodlessly repeated it was clear they came from a wire story and weren't necessarily witnessed by the reporter whose byline appeared on the story: "An egg was thrown at the president's car," noted the *Times*. "An egg was even thrown at Bush's limo," reported *The New York Daily News*. "At one particularly dark moment, a protester lobbed an egg at the presidential limo," it said on Salon.com. "An egg and an orange were thrown at the Bush limousine," said *The New York Post*. And "an egg, four green apples, and a plastic water bottle were tossed in the direction of his limousine," said *The Washington Post*.

All of which, to an eyewitness, verges on ludicrous. I make no pretense of being expert at crowd estimation, for example, and distrust those who say they are—and don't know, either, how anyone could have estimated very precisely the number of people kept dispersed and roaming the streets that day by restrictive security measures—but it was easy to see there was ten thousand people in the deeply integrated crowd merely within a two-block radius of where I stood at 14th and Pennsylvania, from where I also saw the Marines no one reported on, as well as a large amount of refuse thrown at the presidential motorcade (including numerous eggs, perhaps even the famous one).

But what seemed particularly ominous about the coverage was that, across the board, almost no one seemed to make any effort whatsoever to give protest activities the kind of vivid and meaningful presence that even the lavish inaugural balls were given. (A juxtaposition starkly reversed in several British newspapers I also examined online that morning, such as *The Guardian, The Observer, The Times, The Independent*, and *The Daily Telegraph*.)

As I subsequently learned, this proved equally true of the rest of the media octopus. On television, there were a few exceptions—CBS and NBC gave the protests brief although substantive mention. CNN estimated the protestors at a higher number than the official estimate—putting it at about 20,000 people—and showed the occasional, fleeting glimpse of the crowd at 14th and Pennsylvania. But it also showed the thinner crowd of protesters farther down the avenue without reporting that it was thin because all the Checkpoint Charlie entrances in that area had been closed.

On ABC, as Fairness & Accuracy In Reporting (FAIR) detailed on its website, the network's anchor Peter Jennings showed visible and repeated disdain for the protesters. He reported that the thousands of people standing in the freezing rain and hail had "just come for the sake of demonstrating," and that demonstrators were "not spoiling the parade for people at home, but maybe causing resentment among many people at home." This, in between cut-aways to ABCs street reporter Terry Moran, who reported that the demonstrators were a "fringe element" that was "down-right ill-mannered." And while it was not as easy for the television cameras to avoid images of the demonstrators as it had been for the newspapers, the limited visuals were often prevented from speaking for themselves, or replaced entirely by commentary, as when Moran reported that demonstrators bore "very nasty signage" without showing it, and without reporting that "signage" nasty or otherwise had in fact been significantly curtailed by police measures, rendering whatever "signage" was left barely bigger than a sheet of legal paper—i.e., so small as to be unreadable on television.

And television, too, prevailed in misreporting the facts of the most crucial photo-op of them all—the presidential stroll—but to an even greater, and more astonishingly contortionist, degree. On ABC anchorman Jennings noted that it was a "good tradition for the president to get out and be closer to the people," setting up his sidekick commentator Michael Beschloss, a presidential historian, who then asked viewers to imagine if the new president hadn't been able to do that—if he "had had to remain, for security reasons, locked inside that car…." Incredibly, he went on, apparently speaking for himself and Jennings, "I think that would have made a statement that we probably wouldn't have wanted to see."

And there you have it: The statement that had, in fact, been made, had been deemed inappropriate for viewers. Neither Beschloss nor Jennings reported—or perhaps, more frighteningly, understood—that, indeed, the new president had *not* followed the "good tradition" and *had*, in fact, decided to "remain, for security reasons, locked inside that car" until he was beyond the "people" and in a private, barricaded, militarized compound where, as ABCs own Terry Moran put it from within that very compound itself, "The only thing I see are cowboy hats."

It borders on the surreal. And in the shadow of such towering inaccuracy, what happened in the rest of the media, on smaller, local radio and television stations, seemed much more sedate and inconsequential—they either ignored the protests entirely, or broadcast brief and fleeting stories that cited most of the same few details that came up in newspaper reports. (Not so surprising, perhaps: In the age of downsized corporate news, many radio and TV stations feature news known as "rip and read"—that is, taken almost word-for-word from the newspaper or the wires. Thus do newspapers maintain their influence, if not their circulation.)

In subsequent days, of course, no one returned to the story they'd essentially missed in the first place to consider what that gathering of dissenters could signify. Quite the opposite. There seemed to be a determined and almost paternalistic effort by the media to soothe and assure the populace that everything was fine, that the democracy was running smoothly (as if that was the obligation of either print or broadcast journalists); that there was, in any case, no dissent except for that from the usual suspects—the perpetual malcontents, or the troublemaking kids from the Seattle riots, or some such.

By the time, a few days later, *Newsweek* magazine ran a giant version of the photo of the presidential stroll without accurately reporting the circumstances, just like the *Times* and ABC had done before it, the photo seemed to have passed into history as the representative image of the day.

And at the end of the first week of the new administration, on Sunday January 28, not just the fact of the first-ever protest of the presidential transitional process, but the fact of the unprecedented and months-long series of torturous events leading up to that protest, all seemed to have been vaporized

59

when the *Times* declared, in the lead sentence of the lead story on the front page, that it had been "one of the most orderly and politically nimble White House transitions in at least 20 years."

3

THE REVOLUTION WAS
NOT TELEVISED...

Thus do we get an idea of why the crowd lining the parade route in Washington that day shouted "Shame!" at the press trucks... and of course an idea of why those protestors were then ignored. The mutual disdain between the press and its audience became even more evident in the days that immediately followed, when an uproar over the coverage—or lack thereof—broke out amongst the thousands of eyewitnesses just arriving back home from the capital, and there was an immediate flood of reporting and commentary by witnesses in the one place left for them to hold forth: the Internet.

Indeed, the Internet was the place where most of the people who went to Washington that day had learned that there were like-minded souls wanting to organize a protest in the first place. It was where the demonstrations in fact were developed as an idea, gestated, and subsequently organized, all via electronic news letters, e-mail, and homemade websites. It was the place where most of the dozens of attendees that I knew subsequently learned of groups that were going and signed up for bus rides.

And during those weeks leading up to the event, the Internet was a place that positively percolated with optimistic chatter about finally being able to vent the stymied anger over how the president had become the President. People threw themselves into these communications with such gusto that it reminded me of the knowing radicals of the sixties, who did not seem all that bothered when they declared that "The revolution will not be televised."

So it was natural that, when groggy protestors—still achey from the day spent in the freezing rain, still hoarse from their cries of *j'accuse*—got up and saw the newspaper the next morning, the Internet became the place where outrage exploded.

And explode it did: In the week following the protests, outrage over the false and misleading reporting about the inaugural dissent was, for the Internet, what the Kennedy assassination was for television—a moment that redefined the possibilities for, and importance of, the new medium. Suddenly, the Internet was logical, useful, and vitally interesting to an audience exponentially greater than its previous core audience amongst the youth, pornography, and business cultures. And though this moment, too, was grave and seeming to pose a threat to the very nation, it was also, in the fact that it allowed, finally, these ideas to be broached, exciting. People were turning to the Internet for an alternative to mainstream information—a true counterculture was being born, and not just amongst kids or dropouts or modern-day anarchists, but across the full spectrum of American society, including a nervous bourgeoisie.

Two things happened simultaneously: One, detailed accounts of what had actually occurred—including photographs, videos, and audio—broke out on an enormous variety of independent news sites, e-mail newsletters, and individual blogs; simple emails swapping personal narratives were forwarded along and quickly spread like viruses. And two, thousands of furious eyewitnesses launched an attack on the media that had so severely misreported events and in general suppressed the story—an attack that detailed, in effect, the growing sentiment that the mainstream media was as unrepresentative of reality as the new administration.

Of course, herd-leader *The New York Times* came under particularly heavy attack, especially for running the staged photo. The paper was vilified on independent news sites and on numerous media blogs, and was itself besieged with email letters of complaint from the moment its first inaugural coverage appeared the day after the inauguration.

For example, many people responded as did my wife, Valerie Merians—still in her bathrobe, too, that Sunday morning, she stared in growing disbelief at the large, famously crammed front page of the newspaper, which was dedicated in its entirety to the inauguration, and found it inconceivable that the massive tumult she had witnessed was not represented there, that amidst all the thousands of words and large color photographs, only one of the articles (and that, a piece of analysis, not reporting) so much as mentioned that there had been any dissent whatsoever. Infuriated, she immediately sat down and wrote an email to each of the reporters with a front-page byline: Marc Lacey, R. W. Apple Jr., David E. Sanger, and Frank Bruni, the main news reporter for the event, who had his byline on two of the stories. She heard back quickly from Apple—the only one who had, in fact, given mention, albeit brief, to the protestors—and his response was surprising:

> 30 Jan 01
> Dear Ms. Merians,
>
> Thanks for your "e-mail."
> As I am sure you realize, it was my assignment to analyze what went on that day, not to cover the demonstrations or to decide where to put our coverage. That's what I did. But I must confess that I was as stunned as you to see four front-page stories the next day, none of them about the demonstrations, which were mentioned, among the four pieces, only in mine.

A mistake, in my view, and I have sent your letter and several others like it to the powers in New York.

I understand your frustration, having covered demonstrations stretching back to Montgomery in the 1960's.

Best wishes,
R. W. Apple Jr.
Chief Correspondent
The New York Times

Apple's criticism of his own newspaper, his admission that he too was "stunned," was refreshing, and admirable... yet it also made the obliviousness of the other reports—the ones that were, after all, the *news* reports—all the more ominous. In the end, Valerie never did hear back from those "powers," let alone Frank Bruni and the other news reporters.

But as Apple's response suggests, the powers-that-be at *The Times* were under assault. Valerie's letter was only part of the barrage of people castigating the paper for its inaccuracy... and, showing more media savvy than is perhaps expected, the act of not reporting on the demonstrators was generally seen as inaccurate coverage—and asking the obvious question: Why in the world had the *Times* so completely missed such an historically important piece of news?

Less than three weeks after the inauguration, the newspaper had become so overwhelmed with complaints that it issued a blunt and startling response. In a form email sent to various complainants—not all, but, oddly, just those apparently deemed worthy—and subsequently posted on numerous websites such as that of FAIR, "senior news editor" Bill Borders wrote:

> I have your correspondence about our coverage of the protest demonstrations that coincided with the inauguration of President Bush on Jan. 20. I am sorry we disappointed you. But it seems to me that your objection confuses the fact of this, or any, protest demonstration with the events that the demonstrators are protesting against.

The marchers in Washington and elsewhere on Jan. 20 were protesting the irregularities of Bush's election, which we have covered extensively almost every day since Nov. 7. All the Florida electoral peculiarities have been front page news.

In general, we devote more space to events, developments and situations than to demonstrations protesting (or supporting) the events, developments and situations. One reason for this is that the demonstrations are staged events, designed to be covered. So, as we did with this one, we cover them, but modestly. I think our coverage of this demonstration, both on the front page and with the full article inside, was appropriate to the event.

This modest coverage of the demonstration, a staged event, is wholly separate from our coverage of the details of the election. That has been, of course, considerably more substantial.

I assure you that our coverage the Bush presidency will continue to be as vigorous and independent as you might expect. I appreciate your writing, and holding us to a high standard.

Rather than quell anger—or fear—or do anything to tamp down the ominousness of accusations,

Borders's response was an instance of putting out a fire with gasoline: It was an admission that the *Times* had indeed made a deliberate decision not to report on the fact that tens, most likely hundreds, of thousands of people had gathered to question the legitimacy of the Bush inauguration.

Making matters worse was the fact that Borders's reasoning for this decision—that the *Times* does not, as a rule, report on "staged events, designed to be covered"—was severely lacking in terms of not just journalistic ethics but even simple logic: He seemed blithely unaware that the inauguration itself was a staged event—for starters, it took place on an actual stage. The inaugural balls covered in such detail were also, apparently, impromptu. And then there was the staged photo....

In short, it was a response bordering on journalistic dementia. To say that objection to the *Times* poor coverage "confuses the fact of this, or any, protest demonstration with the events that the demonstrators are protesting against," or that a newspaper must give "more space to events, developments and situations than to demonstrations protesting (or supporting) the events, developments and situations," is to expound a philosophy that would have censored coverage of some of the most important events in American history. In the modern era alone, for example, it would have ruled out coverage of such epochal events as the 1963 civil rights march on Washington (the occasion of Martin Luther King's "I have a dream" speech); the Civil Rights march on Selma, Alabama in 1965; the march on the Pentagon in 1967; or the deadly demonstrations at Kent State University in 1970. In fact, it would have ruled out coverage of almost all of the Civil Rights movement—the "demonstrations stretching back to Montgomery in the 1960s" that R. W. Apple so proudly recalled covering—because the *Times* had reported on the relevant legislation. It would have ruled out covering the explosion of riots and protests that took place in the hours after the killing of Martin Luther King, because the *Times* had covered the assassination. It would have ruled out covering the years-long anti–Vietnam War movement in its entirety, because the *Times* had reported on the war.

Yet such was the stated official policy, and for all its Orwellian implications, on the Internet, at least, it inspired a raft of *I told you so*s, as well as a certain charge of encouragement. After all it was a blatant admission from the country's most powerful mainstream media source that it was doing exactly what it was being accused of doing: not reporting on the elephant in the room. Amongst the ignored, this immediately diminished feelings of uncertainty over their paranoia by telling them that they did after all have something to be paranoid about—the press was, indeed, purposefully not reporting on the widespread dissent and unease over the rise of George Bush, which of course then made that continuing rise all the easier. Call it censorship or call it bias in favor of the new right-wing government—in effect it was both, of course—for those who'd shouted "Shame!" just as vociferously at the press trucks as they had at the presidential limo, it was just so much more proof: the press was implicated. As media critic Michael Wolff wrote about coverage of the inauguration in a column that was widely circulated on the Internet (but originated in *New York* magazine, making Wolff one of the few mainstream journalists to comment in any depth on the protests), the days of the reporter as the scruffy, working-class outsider à la the Woodward-Bernstein model were long gone—indeed, Bob Woodward is now far more powerful and certainly richer than most of his subjects, and "The conventional view (the media view of the Washington media) that makes political reporters out to be outsiders and cynical types is almost entirely false; it's the view of another era (a Nixonian era). Political reporters, especially the day-to-day recorders of official Washington developments and events, are protective of Washington. You would not, for instance, get much buy-in to the notion that this—the inauguration of a usurper—is a really wigged-out, psychically destabilizing situation."

Just how "wigged-out" was, however, measured in the aforementioned deluge of reporting that was meanwhile appearing on the Net. Stories hard and soft were posted on some veteran independent news sites, as well as on homemade websites concocted just for the occasion. The websites of non-American newspapers, particularly British newspapers both left and right, were heavily trafficked, as for the most part the rest of the world covered the protests in far greater depth.* Stories were circulated in emailed newsletters both professional and amateur, as well as via collected links to the hard-to-find mainstream stories (such as Michael Wolff's). Most simply of all, stories circulated via the virtual jungle telegraph of email, whereby eyewitnesses and other mainstream media dropouts compared notes and told each other what they'd seen.

One heavily circulated story, for example, was that of the couple that streaked the swearing-in ceremony—supposedly, right in front of the stage as the oath was being pronounced. Given the press

---

*European sources were also among the few who reported on the fact that there were demonstrations by Americans abroad that day, in European capitals such as London and Paris. They were also among the few that reported on the fact that there were sizeable demonstrations, attended by thousands, in other American cities besides Washington, such as Seattle, Portland, San Francisco, and Los Angeles.

presence at the ceremony, it seemed impossible that this could have occurred without being remarked upon anywhere. But as it turned out, the story was true.

Joan Roney, in audio interviews accompanied by photos on both the Democracy Now and Indymedia websites, said some anonymous person had given her and her partner, Matthew Power, tickets for the ceremony when they visited the welcome center the night before. It was too good an opportunity to pass up, said Roney, but the tickets bore warnings that any posters or display items would be confiscated. So, they decided to write messages on their torsos, then strip off their clothes once they got inside. Roney wrote "No Democracy" across her chest, and "Hail to the Thief" on her back, "One person, one vote" on one arm and "Ricky, how could you?" on the other (pop singer Ricky Martin was scheduled to sing at an inaugural party). Powers wore the message, "No Mandate" on his front and "No Prisons" on his back.

Once ensconced in their seats, however, they found they were in a more exclusive area than they'd expected—a mere 30 yards from the podium. Roney told Indymedia, "We were really nervous, and we started panicking," but she explained that "we were concerned more about the people in the audience, about the women and men around us" than about the Secret Service. "There were so many women with dyed ashen blonde hair and furs—tons of furs, tons of heels, and people who were really angry. You could hear a pin drop when Clinton came out, when Gore came out, even when Jimmy Carter came out…. It was very, very scary. It was so very stark and cold and dreary. It was like going to a ceremony where the guards of a concentration camp were celebrating or something…."

Nevertheless, when Supreme Court Justice William Rehnquist stepped forward to issue the oath of office, and George Bush stepped forward to meet him and placed his hand upon the Bible, Roney and Powers stood up in the freezing rain and took off their coats and shirts. Holding hands, they made their way down the aisle and across a platform separating the crowd from the stage.

"People yelled 'Go back to Arkansas!'" said Roney, "and 'I hope you die of pneumonia!' and 'I hope you freeze to death!'" Also from the audience, she added, "There were so many people with video cameras on us."

They were met on the other side of the platform by police and Secret Service agents.

"They said they were going to arrest us, but then they only detained us for about an hour and a half, asking questions and checking our IDs," Roney said in the Indymedia interview. Asked why she'd done it, she said, "I had no choice. With no signs allowed, what can you do?"

Another well-circulated story concerned some-one else prevented from having a protest sign—in this case, a little old lady dressed like a Pilgrim in Union Station, the main train station in the capital.

I first heard about her in an email from a friend, Heidi Schlatter, a 39-year-old video editor. Schlatter wrote that when she and her friends had gone to Union Station to catch a train home after the protests, they found "many people in evening wear filing in to attend an inaugural ball being held there." Simply trying to get to the train platforms, she said, "We were harassed by police," who confiscated their signs so the partiers would not see them. Schlatter said the people in her group were not the only ones so harassed. "One 68-year-old woman dressed very convincingly as a pilgrim was nearly dragged off and arrested for refusing to turn around a sign hanging from her neck. She was surrounded by cops and intimidated until she complied." Gwen Shaffer, a reporter for an alternative news weekly, the *Philadelphia City Paper*, also witnessed the event: She reported that the pilgrim's name was Alice Copeland Brown, and the poster around her neck was a rendering of the goofy, jug-eared cartoon icon of *Mad* magazine, Alfred E. Neuman, made up to look like the new president. Police also harassed Brown about an American flag she was carrying. Brown told Shaffer, "To protest the election, I came dressed as Joan Tilly Hurst, my 15th grandmother," who had come over on the Mayflower. "She came here for freedom, and I can't even walk into a train station," said Brown. "They told me my flag is a weapon!" On the Indymedia site again, I found photos of the incident, and a testimonial written by Brown herself. She said that she was a Southerner, and the last time she had "committed civil disobedience" was "when I integrated lunch counters."

Having encountered few celebrants or supporters of the new administration in my own wide-ranging wanderings around the city that day—save for those tuxedoed and ball-gowned celebrants who'd cursed at us from the buses that were racing to the White House—I was intrigued by the stories of encounters between protestors and jubilant Republicans, of which there were many. For example, someone named James Chance posted a narrative of his day on the Web, saying that as he left the curtailed Supreme Court demonstration, circling the Capitol toward the parade route, he passed "more fur coats, pearls, and color-treated blond hair than I have ever seen in my life," and he offered "quotes [spoken] to myself and my friends from the lovely, polite Texas-type Republicans: 'jackass,' 'suck my nose, bitch,' 'fascist,' 'learn how to vote,' 'sore loser,' 'i wish these people would just go home,' 'freak,' 'get a job,' etc...." Chance also noted that he observed "Republicans constantly trying to get their photos taken with people carrying protest signs and banners, in a bizarre act of exoticism."

There were reports about encounters with the press, too. One writer I know emailed me that he and a companion had confronted a reporter after hearing him report that the protestors "were Nader supporters and would have protested a Gore inauguration as well. We pointed out to him that we would not have protested a Gore inauguration, unless Gore had stolen the election as Bush had."

And it was, ultimately, thanks to the Internet that I finally learned what had happened to the event that had drawn most of us to Washington—

the carefully planned and legally sanctioned march on the Supreme Court building that had mysteriously gone awry. Had the police really broken it up, as the buzz at the protests had it? It seemed to me to be the most sensible, poignant and telling event planned for the day and, determined to find out what had happened, I circulated an email to friends with a message that I asked them to pass on: I'd be interested in hearing from anyone who'd participated in the aborted march. Responses came back quickly, and supplemented what I was reading at independent websites.

One response came from Dare Dukes, a 34-year-old New Yorker who worked as an administrator at the Brennan Center for Justice at the New York University School of Law; he was part of the crowd that left Dupont Circle and headed down P Street. "We filed out of the park with what seemed like a damn big crowd, given that when I climbed a stoop to get a good view I could see neither end of it," he wrote. "The AP story described it as 'hundreds.' Of course, you see what you want in such cases, but many, many folks came out of their houses and businesses to cheer us on. It was pretty inspiring."

"There were many senior citizens there, as well as parents with their young children," wrote Cliff Tisdale, a 50-year-old computer animation designer from Hoboken, New Jersey. "To me, the crowd seemed huge. Surely, big enough to be a major news event." But after the slowly moving crowd had turned on to 14th Street, wrote Tisdale, "a helicopter hovered over us, and then we weren't moving and we didn't know why. We thought maybe we had approached some kind of security checkpoint. In a short time, people were getting anxious. Then we learned that the cross street in front of us, K Street, had been blocked off by police and we were being detained. Chants of 'Let us through' began. Then more and more police started to appear holding clubs and wearing riot helmets. Police formed lines and blocked off the side streets, all the exits. I saw people that were trying to leave, be grabbed by police and pushed back into the crowd. Then, vans pulled up behind us and about 30 police officers formed a human wall and blocked our rear exit as well. We were corralled, unable to continue the march or leave."

According to Dukes, the crowd was defiant at first, "cheering every time the police helicopter hovered overhead, shouting 'Whose Street? Our Street!'; 'Shame!'; etc." But, he wrote, "What eventually transpired was an instructive display of effective crowd control. The crowd eventually became restless and less mobilized, with the back lines straggling off and milling about, wondering what to do."

Tisdale wrote, "I asked a few officers what was going on. No one would give me an answer. One finally told me that there had been violent rioters ahead of us. He said they were throwing garbage cans through windows, smashing property and slashing tires on cars."

Several people suggested I contact David McDermott, a 41-year-old graphic artist from Brooklyn, who was nearer to the front of the line and saw what happened. McDermott didn't want to write about it, but he granted me an interview. He was extremely soft-spoken, with a faint trace of an old Irish brogue. I asked him if he saw the kids throwing garbage cans through windows.

"It wasn't kids throwing trash cans through a window at all," he told me. "A few kids trying to skirt the crowd nudged over a couple of trash bins by the side of the road, and that was it. They just brushed by these trash bins and they fell over. And that was it, you know? They fell over. And the police waded in."

What do you mean "waded in"? I asked.

"Well, they attacked them. The policemen attacked these kids."

They beat them?

"Yeah, they beat them. Using their sticks."

Just for tipping over some trash cans?

"Yeah... It was, it was just complete overkill."

Charles Cohen, a Baltimore-based freelancer who strings for the Reuters wire service and newspapers such as *The Baltimore Sun* and *The*

Washington Post, filed a report on the Indymedia site saying that he'd been south of K Street in an area that "had a deserted police state feel with barricades and watchful cops in all kinds of dress," and was making his way towards Pennsylvania Avenue "when a women pulled up on her bicycle and urged us to go up on 14th Street. People were getting beaten and the cops had trapped some demonstrators. 'They need your support,' she said."

Cohen continued, "We bolted three blocks of no-man's land to come upon chaos. Buses were set up as barricades. A thick crowd of demonstrators were losing their position marching down 14th Street. A wall of cops were forcing them against the east building."

Cohen said he saw a freelance photojournalist he knew, Jeffery Ray, "cradling a broken telescopic lens smashed by a police. Fortunately he already had the footage of a man beaten by cops. He played the stills back for us right there on his digital screen. Ray said the man was on the street and 'they just clubbed him right over the fucking head and he went down and they just kept hitting again until they [the demonstrators] pulled him out.'"

The breakup of the march, however, had an unexpected result for the police—it funneled escapees into another demonstration a few block to the east, in Franklin Park, where, as Indymedia's Eamon Martin reported, a gathering of about 600 members of the mysterious Black Bloc had been surrounded by police, who also had "managed to corral against a building wall about 80 of this group." "Mass arrests seemed imminent" and even pre-planned, Martin reported; the police had come equipped with "loads of plastic, 'zip-tie' handcuffs and City Transity Authority buses" used for "criminal mass transit" awaited nearby.

Dare Dukes escaped the brouhaha at K Street through an alley and found himself at the scene in Franklin Park: "That park seemed to be filled mostly with Black Bloc kids," he wrote in his email. "I say 'kids' because none of these men and women looked much older than 23, and some looked too young to vote. And I won't call them 'anarchists,' the shorthand the media favored in WTO-protest coverage, because there are too many groups to lump together under one ideology and I also never saw the telltale circled 'A' on any of them. One thing was for sure, they were experienced, prepared, worked as a team, and were not afraid of being aggressive, using agit-prop tactics, or facing off with the cops."

Dukes wrote that the police were obviously distracted by the sudden influx of people diverted from 14th Street, which allowed many of the "BBers" to break free of their encirclement. (Many of them would later post thank-you notes on the Web to the Supreme Court marchers for saving them.)

But suddenly, Dukes wrote, while crowds of the Supreme Court marchers continued to gather on the periphery of the park and on the adjacent street corners, "A line of unmarked police passenger vans sped onto the scene, and more cops filed out—these in full riot gear. You couldn't help but feel that things were escalating. A Black Bloc kid—all in black, with a black helmet and ski mask—had climbed a light pole and, twenty feet in the air, unfurled a black banner (I couldn't see the front, so don't know what it said). A kid tapped me on the shoulder and asked me and my friends if we needed vinegar. For what? we asked. He explained that a vinegar-soaked bandana over one's face will neutralize teargas. He said he saw the riot cops donning gas masks, but I didn't see any. Soon BBers and others were pulling from their knapsacks ziplock baggies containing bandanas soaking in vinegar."

Meanwhile, the Black Bloc member on the light pole burned a small American flag, and the police surrounded the base of the pole. Then, according to Duke, "When the kid on the light pole started to inch down, the cops came forward to arrest him once he'd landed. He blew a whistle and shouted 'Black Bloc, Black Bloc!' A bunch of BBers rushed to the base of the pole, and he leaped onto them. They encircled him and swept him away from the cops, while he stripped off his black clothes and helmet and disappeared into the crowd."

But as the growing crowds from the Supreme Court march threatened to join with the Black Bloc demonstrators, "the cops doubled their lines, making it impossible for any of the crowds to reunite with the others," Dukes wrote. "BBers clustered along the line of cops, and, all at once, as if practiced, they shoved forward into the cops. They were beaten back with batons and kicks. This happened repeatedly over about 5 minutes, and things were kind of looking scary at this point. In response to the beatings, the crowd chanted 'You work for us!' at the cops. We saw a kid with a bandaged and bloodied head (the BBers have their own roving team of medics, if you can believe it—all in black except for red crosses on their chests). Press, by the way, at this point, was everywhere. TV cameras, 35mm cameras, swarming the center of the intersection, snapping shots of the flag-burning and the beatings—I was amazed none of this made it into the papers."

Not all of the photojournalists there, however, were able to take pictures—both Charles Cohen and another journalist, photographer Michael Shinn, wrote of being held at bay by police. In a letter to Wired.com, Shinn wrote that he was "basically arrested" when police kept him "and some other reporters pressed up against the wall... even though I had a nice big press badge on."

And so it went: A large march of the bourgeoisie met a rally by a surprisingly large number of well-trained militants in confrontation with the police and a melee ensued, while at least a part of the press corps were physically prevented from reporting the event. Dukes's astonishment seems well-earned: It certainly seems like a story of relevance to the average voter.

And that wasn't the only place where a con-frontation between the Black Bloc and police occurred. At another rally at the Navy Memorial just off Pennsylvania Avenue, another BBer climbed a flagpole, was surrounded by police and leapt off into the waiting arms of his compatriots to escape in the crowd.

This time, however, a photo from a Black Bloc-police confrontation subsequently did make the AP wires (although I found it not in any mainstream publication but on the stalwart Indymedia site). It is an astonishing photograph: A protestor, dressed all in black, with a black mask and even black sneakers, flying with his arms outstretched like Superman above the heads of some boggle-eyed riot cops.

It is, in a way, the opposite of the photo that, it seems decreed, will in history books come to represent the day in iconic fashion: the photo of the president's staged stroll. And it would be easy to say that, in the end, what happened in Washington on the day of George Bush's inauguration comes down to those two photos—one that looks real but is fake, and one that looks fake but is real; one that represents something essential about dissent having to transcend oppression, and one that represents something essential about government and media being, nowadays, more or less in cahoots.

But of course the real story of the day is not so simple. Being in cahoots, as Michael Wolff's comments about media complacency suggest, is not the same thing as a conspiracy (the root of "conspiracist," the term, now come to be derogatory, that both the right and establishment liberals use to dismiss liberals from outside the establishment making these charges). And the protestor flying over the heads of authority is part of the Black Bloc, a group of people who call themselves anarchists, by which they mean rather flippantly—and youthfully—that they are opposed to any concept of rulership, i.e., that they have an ideology of no ideology. It is a notion of detachment that strikes a strange resonance with both the arrogance of the right, and the increasing despair of the left. It resonates, in fact, with something Umberto Eco wrote about the rise of another far-right government—that of media baron Silvio Berlusconi in Italy—which he said represented "the collapse of traditional ideology and its replacement by the populist votes of the mass media." In America, where ideological differences are key to the functioning of the system, this means that a system of checks and balances protecting democracy itself seems, to many, to have failed—first, a vote has been overruled, then the media that was supposed to cover the workings of democracy censored stories on the subsequent unease and dissent.

But in a country founded on dissent against unelected governance, this generates an almost visceral anger. It summons up Baudelaire's comments after the coup by Napolean III that it "has physically depoliticized me. There are no more general ideas," a sentiment which led the poet to declare that he would say of future opportunities to vote, "*Si j'avais voté, je n'aurais pu vote que pour mois.*" ("If I had voted, I could have only voted for myself.")

Is that, then, where this whole affair leaves us— with fewer and fewer people voting, and with the media and elected officials continuing to insist upon apathy as the reason? With the failure to recognize the acceptance of disenfranchisement as a vote in itself? With no one speaking up, because so far as they know, no one else is unhappy?

Time will tell. For now, the fact remains that there is a widely shared perception and widely articulated conviction that democracy in the last election was what was defeated, and in more ways than one. And yet the hopeful fact remains: On January 20, 2001, thousands upon thousands of people descended upon Washington, DC, to stand in a freezing rain and say: This isn't right.

EPILOGUE

"...IT IS PREWAR COVERAGE THAT COUNTS THE MOST."

—MICHAEL GETLER,

THE WASHINGTON POST, 2 MAY 2004

After I completed this report in February of 2001 (and was, not so surprisingly perhaps, unable to place it in any publication), mainstream discussion of the unease over the rise of George W. Bush certainly did not increase. Quite the contrary, what faint discussion there was vaporized entirely a few months later when the September 11 attacks occurred, at which point the mainstream media became even more deferential in its treatment of the new administration.

But the unease continued to be a point of discussion on the Internet, especially when the new administration made clear its unshakeable determination to go to war with Iraq. The fact that a president many felt was illegitimate was taking the country into a war that was so blatantly ill-advised was, to many, the ultimate nightmare scenario of what had gone wrong with our democracy.

Protests continued. But the precedent of the 2000 inaugural day protests was replicated and even further developed: mainstream coverage of dissent showed scant improvement, while the suppressive tactics of controlling and dispersing crowds by municipal authorities and police only intensified.

For example, in New York City on February 15, 2002, another bitterly cold day, police prevented a march of hundreds of thousands of people from gathering at the U.N. for an anti-war rally featuring South African Bishop Desmond Tutu; the avenues and streets surrounding the U.N. were barricaded and people were herded elsewhere. Valerie and I eventually found ourselves herded into a single block with thousands of people, with all areas of egress barricaded by steel barricades and rows of police. People stood packed together, not knowing what to do, when suddenly a squadron of mounted police charged up, waving their billy clubs and shouting at people to get back out of the street. But get back to where? There were far too many people, all them prevented by the barricades from going anywhere. A beat cop standing near me threw up her hands in exasperation at the fear and pandemonium the mounted police were causing; she shook her head and stomped by Valerie and me, quoting, incredibly, John Lennon: "Give peace a chance, man!" she barked as she walked away from a scene edging closer to violence. Meanwhile, the mounted cops seemed nearly deranged, red-faced and screaming, pressing their mounts into the thick, befuddled crowd, the horses terrified and terrifying. When they'd cleared a small opening, one of the cops— screaming, the veins in his neck visible—wheeled his horse around so fast that the horse lost footing on the blacktop and fell on his side. Both horse and rider immediately hopped back to their feet uninjured, and the remounted cop charged off the other way. Here is how the incident was reported in *The New York Post* the next day:

"A police horse was hurt when a protester punched it in the face and dragged it to the ground by its reigns [sic], [Police Commissioner Ray] Kelly added. The horse, Boots, and the riding officer suffered minor injuries."

And so things continued: That protest, at least, made the front pages, but it was the authorities' inaccurate version of things still… after all, who could sympathize with thuggish peaceniks beating up horses?

Thus, while there remained some apparently notable exceptions to the rule, even those exceptions as often as not prove the rule. In a remarkable 2002 interview with the BBC, no less powerful a journalist than Dan Rather, CBS television's counterpart to Peter Jennings, made the case that it is difficult, in the end, to make objective comment. Using what he calls "an obscene comparison," Rather said, "There was a time in South Africa that people would put flaming tires around people's necks if they dissented. And in some ways the fear is that you will be 'necklaced' here, you will have a flaming tire of lack of patriotism put around your neck. Now it is that fear that keeps journalists from asking the toughest of the tough questions. I do not except myself from this criticism. What we are talking about here?

Whether one wants to recognize it or not, or call it by its proper name or not, is a form of self-censorship. I worry that patriotism run amok will trample the very values that the country seeks to defend."

And yet... as I finalize this manuscript for publication, the atrocity of Abu Ghraib prison is slowly coming to light; *The New York Times* is publicly castigating itself for having relied so unquestioningly on administration sources in its reporting on the existence of the still-undiscovered "weapons of mass destruction" used to justify the war against Iraq; and more journalists seem to be sharing Rather's sentiment.

It seems to have finally become unavoidable, in other words, for the media to take seriously the concerns of American protestors, if not the protests themselves—that is, to lessen the paternally dismissive attitude toward dissenters and consider the notion that greater scrutiny and perhaps even criticism of the administration is a more appropriate role for the press in a democracy.

But what of the role of the voters in the political discussion? Despite recent events, there has been no grand revisiting of the issue of the president's legitimacy, nor of why unease was so widely ignored by the mainstream press, why it was even devalued and ridiculed... nor of the question: What would have happened if the dissent had been more seriously considered back in January 2000?

DLJ, 1 June 2004

Except for minor revisions, this report was written in February, 2001. Since then:

THE NEW YORK TIMES... has undergone great turmoil, culminating in several scandals involving plagiarism and faked stories by such staffers as Jayson Blair and Rick Bragg. These scandals led to the ouster of Executive Editor Howell Raines, who was replaced by Bill Keller, and the newspaper has changed from its previous neocon sensibility to a more objective viewpoint that has, noticeably, not hesitated to criticize the ruling administration.

PETER JENNINGS... is still the anchor of ABC News.

INDYMEDIA... is still an active and popular online publication, with a readership that has grown considerably thanks in large part to its protest coverage. It now has branches that cover specific localities, such as the DCIndymedia.com site.

MICHAEL BESCHLOSS... continues to be a regular commentator on television news programs, being, for example, a "regular contributor" on PBS television's *The NewsHour* with Jim Lehrer. His bio on the PBS website notes that he continues to publish books about presidential history, that he holds appointments from the Smithsonian Institution, as well as Harvard and Oxford, and that he lives in Washington with his wife, Afsaneh Beschloss, a World Bank executive.

BILL BORDERS... is still a senior editor at *The New York Times*, and is still, often, the person who writes the response to those who criticize the paper.

R. W. APPLE JR.... has written less and less news commentary for the *Times* since his inaugural analysis. His infrequent writings for the newspaper now are mostly about food or travel or cultural matters.

DAVID E. SANGER... continues to write front page news stories for *The New York Times*, although a May 30, 2004 column by the newspaper's ombudsman, Daniel Okrent, criticized him for not being "aggressive" enough in a front page story portraying a Bush administration source on the existence of weapons of mass destruction in Iraq.

FRANK BRUNI... is still at *The New York Times*. He is now a restaurant critic.

GEORGE W. BUSH... led the country to war after the 9/11 attacks, less than a year after he was inaugurated. He led the country into a second war a year later. Both wars are still going on as this book goes to press.

Black Bloc protestor and police at the U.S. Navy Memorial

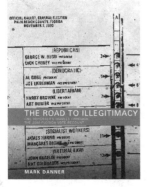

THE ROAD TO ILLEGITIMACY
**One Reporter's Travels Through
the 2000 Florida Vote Recount**
Mark Danner

0-9749609-6-9
$8.95 US / $12.95 CAN

In a masterful work of investigative journalism, *New Yorker* staffer Mark Danner looks into the tense counting and recounting of votes in Florida with a revealing on-the-scene account of the near-hysterical partisan bickering over each and every ballot. What he uncovers is shocking—and his riveting account is a sobering consideration of the question the Supreme Court left hanging: Who actually got the most votes?

IRREPARABLE HARM
**The U.S. Supreme Court and the Decision
That Made George W. Bush President**
Renata Adler

0-9749609-5-0
$8.95 US / $12.95 CAN

In a blistering, no-holds-barred analysis, acclaimed writer Renata Adler uncovers numerous problems with the Supreme Court's decision in *Bush v. Gore.* Adler, herself an attorney, uncovers instances where the judges seem to have miscited their own previous decisions… examines what was said by attorneys and judges in the courtroom… and, ultimately, reveals what really happened in this historic case.

THE BIG CHILL
**The Great, Unreported Story of
the Bush Inauguration Protest**
Dennis Loy Johnson

0-9749609-7-7
$8.95 US / $12.95 CAN

An enormous, angry crowd lined the parade route for George Bush's inauguration, causing him to abandon the traditional walk along Pennsylvania Avenue. Yet a photo of a walking Bush appeared in newspapers the next day. In a gripping first-hand report, Johnson reveals what really happened in Washington: the enormous military presence, the violence between police and protestors, how the Bush photo was staged—and why the historic protest was ignored.